Going to Day Care

FISHER · PRICE
Parking Ramp · Service Center
ELEVATOR
STOP

FIRST EXPERIENCES

Going to Day Care

BY FRED ROGERS

photographs by Jim Judkis

G.P. PUTNAM'S SONS
New York

With special thanks to: Nan Earl Newell, Research; Margaret B. McFarland, Ph.D., Senior Consultant; the Carnegie-Mellon University Child Care Center; Rachel Nora Linke Pisciotta, Henry Pisciotta and Erika Linke; Margaret Wyler; and all of the parents and children who agreed to help us with the book.

 Published simultaneously in
Canada by General Publishing Co. Limited, Toronto.
Printed in the United States of America
Production assistance: Cathy Cohen Droz
Book design by Kathleen Westray
Library of Congress Cataloging in Publication Data
Rogers, Fred. Going to day care.
(Mister Rogers' neighborhood—a first experiences book)
At head of title: Mister Rogers' neighborhood.
Summary: Describes the typical activities and feelings
children can experience at a day care center, including the
conflicts and apprehensions involved in being away from home,
along with the fun and excitement.
1. Day care centers—Juvenile literature. I. Judkis, Jim, ill.
II. Mister Rogers' neighborhood (Television program)
III. Title. IV. Series.
HV851.R64 1985 362.7'12 84-24940
ISBN 0-399-21235-3
ISBN 0-399-21237-X (pbk.)
Third impression

For more and more young children, day care—rather than preschool or kindergarten—is becoming the first major separation from home.

For many parents day care is a necessity, but even those who put their very young children in day care by choice have mixed feelings about what that separation may mean. Most parents find separation easier to cope with when they feel good about the people who will be looking after their child and about the place where their child will be. Finding a day-care situation that feels "just right" may take a lot of time and effort, but I believe you'll find that time and effort worthwhile—for both you and your child.

Talking candidly with your child about going to day care can help lessen his or her anxious feelings about being away from you. When children are reassured that they *will* come home at the end of the day, they can often find more enjoyment in all that happens during your times apart. And letting them know how much they are loved and valued at home can help them develop healthy, trusting attachments to the new adults who will be looking after them in day care.

—Fred Rogers

When children are at home, their parents
take care of them in many different ways
because they love them.

They make sure they eat good food.
They make sure they get enough sleep.
They read to them and help them to learn
new things.

Can you think of ways your mom or dad
takes care of you?

When moms and dads have to be away from home at the same time, they need to find other grown-ups who will take care of their children. These grown-ups are sometimes called day-care givers because they give care during the day. Parents and day-care givers get to know each other well. They talk about what children need for good care away from home.

Sometimes children go to places called day-care centers

or to day-care givers' homes. They go there during the day until it's time to go home. There are many different kinds of day-care places, but they all have grown-ups who want to take care of children.

Is there someone special who takes care of you when your mom or dad needs to be away for a while?

Children can have many different feelings about going to day care. At first, they may not be sure they want to stay, or they may not want their mom or dad to leave. Sometimes it's hard to say good-bye to your parents even when you know they will come back for you later. How do you feel when your mom or dad has to leave you for a while?

The grown-ups at day care understand those feelings because they know a lot about children. And they were little once too!

Many things at day care are different from home, but many things are a lot alike. There are places for children to put their own things. They can bring something from home if they want to.

Is there something special you like to take with you when you go away from home?

There are toys to play with. Sometimes it's hard to share with the other children, but the grown-ups there make sure everyone has a turn.

There is a kitchen . . .

and there is a bathroom.

Some younger children may be wearing diapers, but older children can always go to the bathroom any time they need to. Some day-care centers even have small toilets just the right size for children.

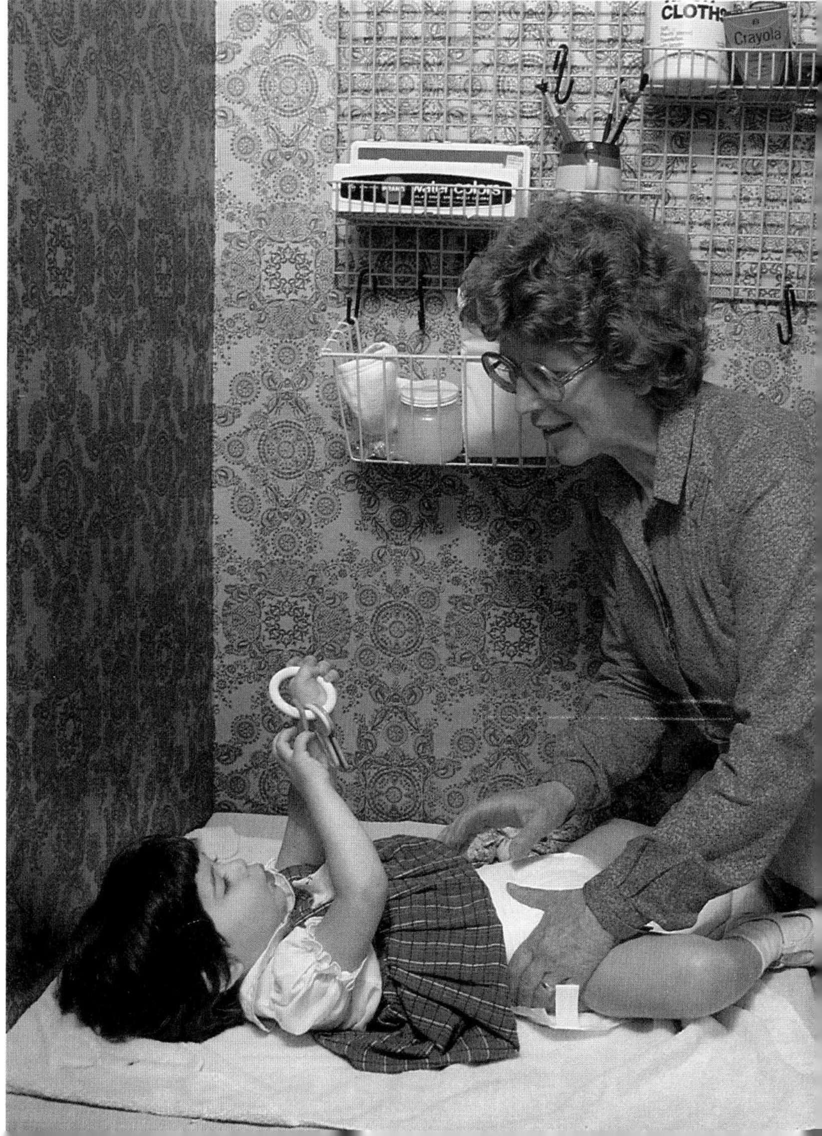

There are some things children can do all by themselves . . .

and there are some things children need help with. Sometimes you have to wait for a grown-up to help you. Grown-ups can often seem very busy. Waiting is hard for everyone—even for grown-ups—but learning to wait is an important part of growing.

Children can help grown-ups too.

And children can help other children. When they help younger children, they sometimes feel like they're playing Mom and Dad. Do you ever help take care of someone younger than you?

There are times during the day to do different things. There is a time for playing inside . . .

and, if the weather's good enough, a time for playing outside.

There is a time for being together . . .

and a time for being alone.

There is a time for being with a friend . . .

and a time for talking about important things with a grown-up. If you're feeling sad or angry or especially happy about something, you might want to tell a grown-up about it.

It feels good to know that there are times when you can have someone you love all to yourself.

There are snack times and a time for lunch. At some day-care places children bring their own food from home. At other places the grown-ups fix snacks and lunch right there—and sometimes children can help. It can be fun to eat together.

There is a time to be quiet, and there are places to lie down. Nobody has to go to sleep during nap time, but some children do.

There is a time for listening to stories . . .

and a time for making up your own.

There is a time for drawing or painting or other things like that.

Sometimes children make things to give to their parents because they like to think about their moms and dads during the day. Parents often think about their children during the day too.

There is a time to clean up and a time to put things away, and a time to get ready to go home.

Then there is a time to *go* home. The grown-ups at day care are proud of what children have done during the day, and they like to talk about those things with parents.

At the end of the day it feels good to be home. Parents are proud of the way their children are learning to play by themselves and to play with others. There's a lot to talk about.

Can you think of something you might want to tell the people you love about your day today . . . and something you might want to ask them about theirs?